MY FIRST BOOK ABOUT

KANSAS

by Carole Marsh

This activity book has material which correlates with the Kansas Core Content for Assessment. At every opportunity, we have tried to relate information to the History and Social Science, English, Science, Math, Civics, Economics, and Computer Technology CCA directives. For additional information, go to our websites: **www.kansasexperience.com** or **www.gallopade.com**.

Gallopade is proud to be a member of these educational organizations and associations:

The Kansas Experience Series

My First Pocket Guide to Kansas!

The Big Kansas Reproducible Activity Book

The Kansas Coloring Book!

Kansas "Jography!": A Fun Run Through Our State

Kansas Jeopardy: Answers & Questions About Our State

The Kansas Experience! Sticker Pack

The Kansas Experience! Poster/Map

Discover Kansas CD-ROM

Kansas "GEO" Bingo Game

Kansas "HISTO" Bingo Game

A Word... From the Author

Do you know when I think children should start learning about their very own state? When they're born! After all, even when you're a little baby, this is your state too! This is where you were born. Even if you move away, this will always be your "home state." And if you were not born here, but moved here—this is still your state as long as you live here.

We know people love their country. Most people are very patriotic. We fly the U.S. flag. We go to Fourth of July parades. But most people also love their state. Our state is like a mini-country to us. We care about its places and people and history and flowers and birds.

As a child, we learn about our little corner of the world. Our room. Our home. Our yard. Our street. Our neighborhood. Our town. Even our county.

But very soon, we realize that we are part of a group of neighbor towns that make up our great state! Our newspaper carries stories about our state. The TV news is about happenings in our state. Our state's sports teams are our favorites. We are proud of our state's main tourist attractions.

From a very young age, we are aware that we are a part of our state. This is where our parents pay taxes and vote and where we go to school. BUT, we usually do not get to study about our state until we are in school for a few years!

So, this book is an introduction to our great state. It's just for you right now. Why wait to learn about your very own state? It's an exciting place and reading about it now will give you a head start for that time when you "officially" study our state history! Enjoy,

Carole Marsh

Let's Make Words!

Make as many words as you can from the letters in the words:

Kansas,
THE SUNFLOWER STATE!

_____ _____ _____

_____ _____ _____

_____ _____ _____

_____ _____ _____

_____ _____ _____

_____ _____ _____

_____ _____ _____

_____ _____ _____

_____ _____ _____

_____ _____ _____

Kansas
The 34th State

Do you know when Kansas became a state? Kansas became the 34th state on January 29, 1861.

Color Kansas red. Color the Atlantic and the Pacific oceans blue. Color the rest of the United States shown here green.

Pacific Ocean

Atlantic Ocean

KS

N
NW   NE
W   E
SW   SE
S

State Flag

Kansas' current state flag was adopted in 1927. It features a sunflower atop the state seal on a blue background. Under the sunflower, there is a blue and gold bar. In 1961, the word Kansas was added to the flag at the bottom.

Color Kansas' state flag below.

KANSAS

I pledge allegiance...

Kansas
State Bird

Most states have a state bird. It should remind us that we need to "fly high" to achieve our goals. The Kansas state bird is the western meadowlark. It is yellow breasted with a black "V" on its chest. It has brown feathers with white outer tail feathers.

Circle the Kansas state bird, then color all the birds.

The early bird gets the worm! *Yikes!*

Mockingbird

Western Meadowlark

Cardinal

Eagle

Quail

Robin

The state motto is: *Ad Astra per Aspera.* It means "To the Stars through Difficulties."

In 25 words or less, explain what this motto means:

_____

_____

_____

_____

The state seal of Kansas shows a landscape with the sun rising. There is a steamboat on a river and a man plowing in a field. Heading west is a wagon train, and two Native Americans are chasing buffalo. There is a cluster of 34 stars at the top.

Color the state seal.

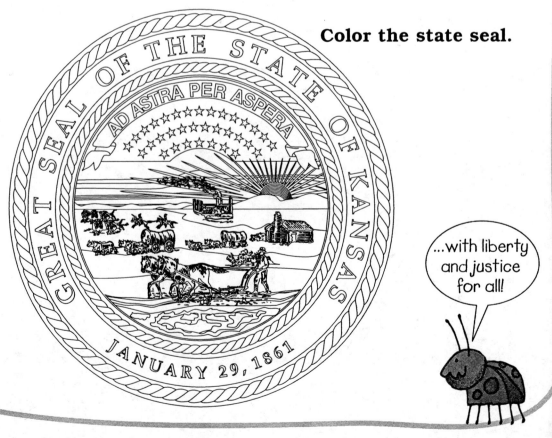

...with liberty and justice for all!

Kansas
State Flower

Every state has a favorite flower. Kansas' state flower is the sunflower. They can grow from 2–6 feet (0.6–1.8 meters) in height. The flower head is made up of ray and disk flowers. The disks can be either brown or yellow. The rays are yellow.

Color the pictures of the Kansas state flower.

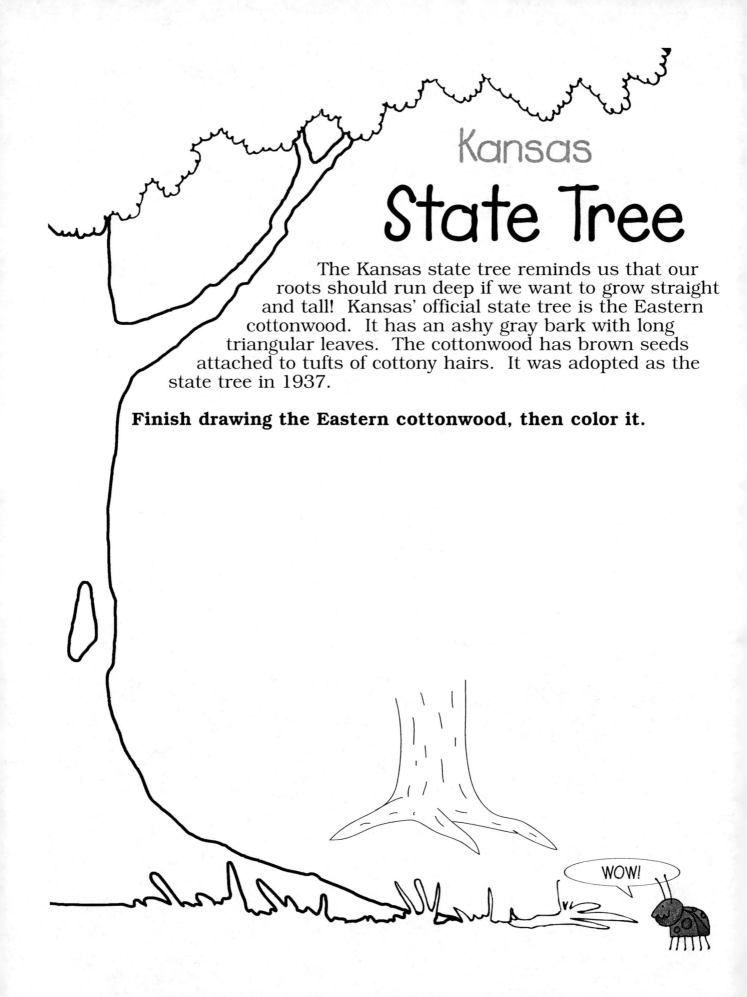

Kansas
State Tree

The Kansas state tree reminds us that our roots should run deep if we want to grow straight and tall! Kansas' official state tree is the Eastern cottonwood. It has an ashy gray bark with long triangular leaves. The cottonwood has brown seeds attached to tufts of cottony hairs. It was adopted as the state tree in 1937.

Finish drawing the Eastern cottonwood, then color it.

WOW!

Kansas
State Zoo

Caney is home to Safari Zoological Park. It has over 100 different species of animals; including big cats, monkeys, llamas, and snakes.

Match the name of the zoo animal with its picture.

Zebra

Giraffe

Chimpanzee

Bear

Tiger

State Explorers

In 1541, Spanish explorers reached Kansas, in search of gold. In 1682, France explored and claimed Kansas as their own. In 1803, Kansas territory became part of the United States. Meriwether Lewis and William Clark then explored the area on their way to the Pacific Ocean.

Circle the things an explorer might have used.

Let's go exploring!

Kansas
State Insect

The honeybee is Kansas' state insect. The honeybee became the state insect in 1976. It is very important to the success of the crops in Kansas. Farmers are aware of the honeybee's importance for pollinating the plants that produce the crops.

Put an X by each critter that is not a honeybee and then color them all!

One Day I Can Vote!

When you are 18 and register according to state laws, you can vote! So please do! Your vote counts!

Your friend is running for a class office.

Here is her opponent!

She gets 41 votes!

He gets 16 votes!

ANSWER THE FOLLOWING QUESTIONS:

1. Who won?   ❏ friend   ❏ opponent

2. How many votes were cast altogether?

3. How many votes did the winner win by?

Kansas
State Capital

Topeka became the state capital of Kansas in 1861. Topeka was chosen to be a railroad center in the early days of its settlement. It was also considered to be a "free-soil" center for those who fought slavery in the region. The capitol building was built of native limestone in 1866.

Add your hometown to the Kansas map.

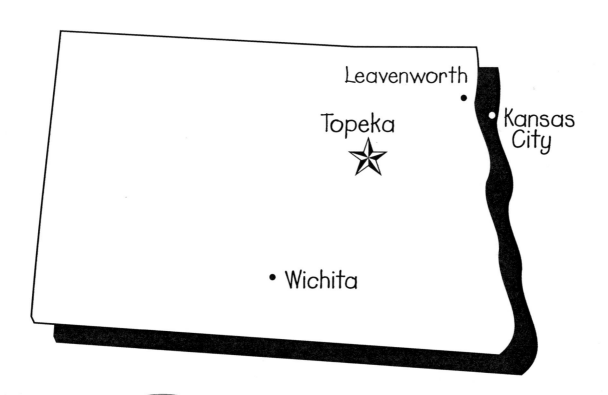

Kansas
Governor

The governor of Kansas is the state's leader.
Do some research to complete this biography of the governor

Governor's name:

_____

Paste a picture of the
governor in the box.

The governor was born in
this state:

_____

The governor has been in office since:

_____

Names of the governor's family members:

_____

_____

_____

Interesting facts about the governor:

_____

_____

_____

_____

_____

Kansas
Crops

Some families in Kansas make their living from the land. Some of the state's crops or farm products are:

WORD BANK

Wheat   Corn   Hogs

Oats   Sunflowers   Barley

UNSCRAMBLE THESE IMPORTANT STATE CROPS

eatwh_____

toas_____

leyarb_____

ronc _____

owflnusers_____

ghos _____

Kansas
State Holidays

These are just some of the holidays that Kansas celebrates.

Number these holidays in order from the beginning of the year.

Columbus Day 2nd Monday in October	Thanksgiving 4th Thursday in November	Presidents' Day 3rd Monday in February
Independence Day July 4	Labor Day first Monday in September	New Year's Day January 1
Memorial Day last Monday in May	Veterans Day November 11	Christmas December 25

Nickname

Kansas has a very special nickname. It is called The Sunflower State.

What other nicknames would suit Kansas and why?

_____

_____

_____

_____

What nicknames would suit your town or your school?

_____

_____

_____

_____

_____

_____

What's your nickname?

Nick.

How BIG is the State?

Kansas ranks 15th in size in the United States. It has a total (land and water) area of 82,282 square miles (213,109 square kilometers).

Can you answer the following questions?

1. How many states are there in the United States?

   _____

2. How many states are smaller than Kansas?

   _____

3. How many states are larger than Kansas?

   _____

Bigfoot was here!

ANSWERS: 1-50; 2-35; 3-14

Kansas
People

    A state is not just towns, mountains, and rivers. A state is its people! Some really important people in a state are not always famous. You may know them—they may be your mom, your dad, or your teacher. The average, everyday person is the one who makes the state a good state. How? By working hard, by paying taxes, by voting, and by helping Kansas children grow up to be good state citizens!

Match each Kansan with his or her accomplishment.

1. George Brett

2. Buffalo Bill Cody

3. Colonel Henry Leavenworth

4. Bob Dole

5. Dwight D. Eisenhower

A. Famous Wild West figure

B. U.S. representative and senator for Kansas

C. Kansas baseball legend

D. Started Fort Leavenworth settlement

E. 34th president of the United States

ANSWERS: 1-C; 2-A; 3-D; 4-B; 5-E;

Kansas
Gazetteer

A gazetteer is a list of places.

Use the word bank to complete the names of some of these famous places in Kansas:

1. Little __ __ __ __ __ on the Prairie

2. Old Abilene __ __ __ __

3. __ __ __ __ Riley

4. Safari Zoological __ __ __ __

5. Kansas Cosmosphere and __ __ __ __ __ Center

WORD BANK

Town   Park
Space   Fort
House

Kansas
Neighbors

No person or state lives alone. You have neighbors where you live. Sometimes they may be right next door. Other times, they may be way down the road. You live in the same neighborhood and are interested in what goes on there.

You have neighbors at school. The children who sit in front, beside, or behind you are your neighbors. You may share books. You might borrow a pencil. They might ask you to move so they can see the board better.

We have a lot in common with our state neighbors. Some of our land is alike. We share some history. We care about our part of the country. We share borders. Some of our people go there; some of their people come here. Most of the time we get along with our state neighbors. Even when we argue or disagree, it is a good idea for both of us to work it out. After all, states are not like people—they can't move away!

Use the color key to color Kansas and its neighbors.

Color Key:

Kansas-red
Nebraska-yellow
Colorado-green
Missouri-orange
Oklahoma-purple
Missouri River-blue

Kansas
Highs and Lows

Kansas' highest point is Mount Sunflower, at 4,039 feet (1,231 meters) above sea level.

Draw a picture of a family climbing Mount Sunflower.

The lowest point in Kansas is the Verdigris River, at 680 feet (207 meters) above sea level.

Draw a picture of a boating scene on the Verdigris River.

Old Man River

Kansas has many great rivers. Rivers give us water for our crops. Rivers are also water "highways." On these water highways travel crops, manufactured goods, people, and many other things—including children in tire tubes!

Here are some of Kansas's most important rivers:

- Kansas River
- Cimarron River
- Neosho River
- Arkansas River
- Verdigris River
- Solomon River

Draw a kid "tubing" down the Arkansas River!

Kansas
Weather ... Or Not!

What kind of climate does Kansas have? Kansas' temperatures can drop to 30°F (–1°C) in the winter and reach 78°F (26°C) in the summer. Snow and ice is common in the winter months, while tornadoes are frequent in spring and summer months.

You might think adults talk about the weather a lot. But Kansas weather is very important to the people of the state. Crops need water and sunshine. Weather can affect Kansas industries. Good weather can mean more money for the state. Bad weather can cause problems that cost money.

ACTIVITY: Do you watch the nightly news at your house? If you do, you might see the weather report. Tonight, turn on the weather report. The reporter talks about the state's regions, cities, towns, and neighboring states. Watching the weather report is a great way to learn about the state. It also helps you know what to wear to school tomorrow!

What is the weather outside now? Draw a picture.

Kansas
Indian Tribes

The American Indians were first on our land, long before it was a state. Kansas' main Indian tribes include:

COMANCHE   KIOWA   CHEYENNE

ARAPAHO

Help Maize find her way through the maize (corn) field maze to her hut made of saplings!

Start

Finish

Kansas
Website Page

Here is a website you can go to and learn more about Kansas:

www.50states.com

Design your own state website page on the computer screen below.

State Song

The official state song for Kansas is "Home on the Range."
Below is the chorus:

"Home on the Range"
composed by Brewster Higley
and Daniel Kelley

Home, home on the range,
Where the deer and the antelope play,
Where seldom is heard a discouraging word,
And the skies are not cloudy all day.

**How does the state song make you feel? Write a verse
about something in Kansas that means a lot to you.**

_____

_____

_____

_____

_____

_____

_____

_____

_____

Kansas
State Animal

The Kansas state animal is the buffalo. The American buffalo was adopted as the state animal in 1955. It is the largest wild animal in America. Bison is another name for buffalo.

Draw six buffalo on the prairie below. Color each one.

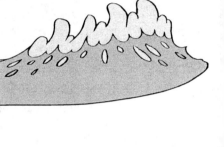

Kansas
Spelling Bee!

What's All The Buzz About?

Here are some words related to Kansas.

See if you can find them in the Word Search below.

WORD LIST

STATE	RIVER	PEOPLE	TREE	BIRD
FLAG	VOTE	FLOWER	SONG	INSECT

```
A  X  N  Y  H  N  V  S  D  G  T  R  E  P
V  O  T  E  M  A  C  S  E  A  B  A  Y  E
S  N  B  R  X  B  R  K  S  X  B  D  S  O
Y  B  P  Q  L  S  O  N  G  R  I  J  H  P
R  I  V  E  R  P  P  L  R  T  Y  U  E  L
Q  R  E  R  R  Y  Z  E  E  R  T  O  N  E
R  D  P  P  A  E  A  O  N  E  C  K  A  R
S  X  O  C  E  A  W  C  T  C  E  S  N  I
P  O  B  U  Y  U  Y  O  E  O  L  L  D  O
Q  U  F  L  A  G  R  K  L  L  X  Z  O  P
Z  X  R  D  G  H  R  E  U  F  L  L  A  L
M  R  D  W  Q  N  M  N  S  T  A  T  E  Z
```

Kansas
Trivia

A ball of twine in Cawker City measures more than 38 feet (11.6 meters) in circumference and is still growing.

Hutchinson has a grain elevator that is a half-mile (0.8-kilometer) long and holds 46 million bushels of grain.

Dodge City is the windiest city in the United States.

Ice cream and cherry pie were against the law in Kansas at one time.

There are 27 towns named Walnut Grove in Kansas.

A hailstone weighing 1.5 pounds (0.68 kilograms) once fell on Coffeyville.

Medicine bundles were sacred to Native Americans. They were used in important ceremonies and rituals.

Russell Stover was born in Kansas. He gave us the Eskimo Pie and Russell Stover candies.

The COWBOY Society (Cock-eyed Old West Band of Yahoos) of the Old West was formed to preserve the cowboy stories of Kansas.

The sea of prairie land is called "The Grassland Sea." It is home to more than 10 million insects per acre (0.4 hectare).

Garden City is home to the world's biggest hairball. It was found in a cow's stomach at the packing plant.

Now add a fact you know about Kansas here:

_____

_____

_____